Write Your Recovery

THE SOBER(ISH) EARLY SOBRIETY JOURNAL

By Alicia Gilbert

ISBN: 9781086491166

I am not a medical professional and this journal should not be
taken as medical advice

Fall down seven times, stand up eight.

- Japanese Proverb

Table of Contents

HOW TO USE THIS JOURNAL

- This book is to help you navigate the early days of sobriety.

- The primary section contains 18 prompts and workbook pages to help you get a handle on WHY you've decided to get sober, its impact on your life, the effects of your drinking, and motivation to help you move forward on tough days.

- You do not need to go in order.

- Use prompts and pages that apply to you. Ignore those that don't.

- Included in this guide are 14 bonus prompts and workbook pages to help you deal with slip ups and relapse and get back on track with your sobriety.

Prompts

FOR EARLY SOBRIETY

PROMPT #1

Why do you want to quit drinking alcohol?

Really think this one through. What has brought you to this point? Start writing down any reason you can think. No reason is too small. Put it all out there.

Today's Date: _____

_____

_____

_____

_____

_____

_____

_____

_____

_____

_____

_____

PROMPT #2

How would your life be different if you were sober?

Use your imagination. Allow yourself a bit of hope and optimism here. What would change about your life if you stop drinking and what would it mean to you?

Today's Date: _____

_____

_____

_____

_____

_____

_____

_____

_____

_____

_____

PROMPT #3

What excites you the most about sobriety? What scares you?

It's okay to feel a mixture of excitement, fear, and everything in between when you first quit drinking. It's normal.

The best way to handle these conflicting emotions is to dump them onto a page where you can process them more clearly.

Today's Date: _____

_____

_____

_____

_____

_____

_____

_____

_____

_____

_____

_____

_____

_____

_____

_____

_____

_____

_____

_____

_____

_____

_____

_____

_____

_____

_____

_____

_____

_____

_____

PROMPT #4

What does sobriety mean for you and your life?

What's at stake here? If you can get and stay sober, what would that mean for you? How would it change your internal and external world?

Today's Date: _____

_____

_____

_____

_____

_____

_____

_____

_____

_____

_____

WRITE YOUR RECOVERY

PROMPT #5

What are your TOP 5 reasons for getting sober?

Today's Date: _____

#1 _____

_____

_____

#2 _____

_____

_____

#3 _____

_____

_____

19

#4 _____

_____

_____

#5 _____

_____

_____

Why did you choose these reasons?

_____

_____

_____

_____

_____

_____

_____

_____

_____

_____

_____

PROMPT #6

Who would your sobriety impact the most and why?

Include as many people in this response as you want. Don't forget about yourself.

Today's Date: _____

_____

_____

_____

_____

_____

_____

_____

_____

_____

_____

_____

_____

_____

_____

_____

_____

_____

_____

_____

_____

_____

_____

_____

_____

_____

_____

_____

_____

_____

PROMPT #7

My life has value because…

Today's Date: _____

_____

_____

_____

_____

_____

_____

_____

_____

_____

_____

_____

_____

_____

_____

_____

_____

_____

_____

_____

_____

_____

_____

_____

_____

_____

_____

_____

_____

_____

_____

_____

_____

PROMPT #8

I want to change my life because…

Today's Date: _____

_____

_____

_____

_____

_____

_____

_____

_____

_____

_____

_____

_____

_____

_____

_____

_____

_____

_____

_____

_____

_____

_____

_____

_____

_____

_____

_____

_____

_____

_____

_____

PROMPT #9

If I could wave a magic wand...

Today's Date: _____

_____

_____

_____

_____

_____

_____

_____

_____

_____

_____

_____

_____

_____

PROMPT #10

I deserve a happy, healthy life because...

Today's Date: _____

_____

_____

_____

_____

_____

_____

_____

_____

_____

_____

_____

_____

_____

_____

_____

_____

_____

_____

_____

_____

_____

_____

_____

_____

_____

_____

_____

_____

_____

_____

_____

Workbook Section

In this section, you'll continue to grapple with some big ideas and questions. Just in a slightly different format.

WORKSHEET #1

When you think about sobriety what are your hopes and fears?

Use the chart below to make a list of anything that scares you or brings you hope about sobriety. Write whatever comes to mind. Don't try to filter your ideas.

HOPES	FEARS

WORKSHEET #2

It's time to make a plan for handling your triggers in sobriety.

A trigger is anything that will tempt you to drink. Take some time to identify your drinking triggers and what you can do to avoid or overcome them.

There will be additional space on the next page if you need it. Try to think of as many things as possible.

Trigger	How I plan to handle it

Trigger	How I plan to handle it

User note: come back and update this list as you learn more about what triggers your drinking. It's a helpful tool in keeping you on track.

WORKSHEET #3

List all the ways you can relax, manage stress, and decompress without alcohol.

One of the biggest drinking triggers for people is stress. Now that you've stopped drinking, how do you plan to take the edge off a tough day?

WORKSHEET #4

The Quit List

What do you plan to quit in order to make sobriety work? List them below.

Example: I'm going to quit going to happy hour on Fridays.

WORKSHEET #5

Creating a support plan.

Which support networks, programs, and loved ones will you be utilizing on your sobriety journey?

Check the ones you plan to use and commit to starting.

	AA, SMART Recovery, or other in-person sobriety group
	Rehab (in-patient or out-patient)
	Online sobriety meetings (ex. In The Rooms)
	Online sobriety support groups (ex. Sober FB groups)
	Religious or spiritual advisor
	Talk therapy or other counseling (in-person or remote)
	Other:

What is your start date?

_____

Who will help hold you accountable?

_____

WORKSHEET #6

Who's on your team?

A strong support plan includes identifying your go-to people for sobriety support. This is your team. Anybody who is a positive influence and/or resource for you at this time is a team member.

List them here and what you need from them.

Team Member	What I need from him/her...

WORKSHEET #7

If nothing changes, nothing changes.

What are you going to change in order to make your sobriety work?
List them out below.

I'm going to change....

WORKSHEET #8

Taking out the trash

There's a trashcan in the corner of this page. What do you plan to throw in there to make sobriety work?

BONUS SECTION: WHAT IF YOU DRINK AGAIN?

Managing Slip-Ups & Relapse

If you make a mistake and drink again, there are a few things you need to know:

1. It is normal.
2. It doesn't mean you can't get sober.
3. All you have to do is start over.

This section will help you stand back up. Mistakes happen. You have the power to make sure they don't happen again.

PROMPT #11

Why did you drink? What happened?
What triggered your drinking?

Today's Date: _____

_____

_____

_____

_____

_____

_____

_____

_____

_____

_____

_____

_____

_____

_____

_____

_____

_____

_____

_____

_____

_____

_____

_____

_____

_____

_____

_____

_____

_____

_____

PROMPT #12

What feelings do you have since drinking? Where do these feelings come from?

Today's Date: _____

_____

_____

_____

_____

_____

_____

_____

_____

_____

_____

_____

_____

_____

PROMPT #13

Complete the sentence and keep going.
"I made a mistake, but it doesn't define
me. I know now that..."

Today's Date: _____

_____

_____

_____

_____

_____

_____

_____

_____

_____

_____

_____

_____

_____

PROMPT #14

How could you have handled this trigger differently? What lesson did you learn that will help you stay sober in the future?

Today's Date: _____

_____

_____

_____

_____

_____

_____

_____

_____

_____

_____

_____

_____

_____

_____
_____
_____
_____
_____
_____
_____
_____
_____
_____
_____
_____
_____
_____
_____
_____
_____

PROMPT #15

What is one thing you will do today to recommit to your sobriety?

Today's Date: _____

_____

_____

_____

_____

_____

_____

_____

_____

_____

_____

_____

_____

_____

_____

_____

_____

_____

_____

_____

_____

_____

_____

_____

_____

_____

_____

_____

_____

_____

_____

_____

_____

_____

DEALING WITH YOUR INNER A**HOLE

Think about the inner voice that is constantly negotiating with you and bringing you down. It talks you into drinking. It tells you lies about what kind of person you are.

That voice is your inner a**hole and it does not want anything good for you.

We're going to work on how to deal with it.

WORKSHEET #9

Create an avatar for that inner voice that is always trying to get you in trouble.

What's your inner a**hole's name?

_____

What words best describe him/her?

_____

What kind of things does your inner a**hole say to you?

_____

_____

_____

_____

If your inner a**hole was a real-life person, what would s/he look like? How would s/he behave? What kind of personality would s/he have?

You can write about it or make a sketch. Whatever suits your creativity.

WORKSHEET #10

Write a letter to your inner a**hole.

What do you want him/her to know?

Dear _____,

_____

_____

_____

_____

_____

_____

_____

_____

_____

_____

_____

_____

WORKSHEET #11

Proving your inner a**hole wrong.

Let's look at everything your inner a**hole says to you and why s/he is wrong.

Crazy stuff my inner a**hole says	Why s/he is wrong

WORKSHEET #12

The role of your inner a**hole in your decision to drink again.

What role did that critical, inner voice play in your decision to drink again? What kind of things did s/he say?

What's a better way to handle this in the future?

_____

_____

_____

_____

_____

_____

_____

_____

_____

_____

_____

_____

WORKSHEET #13

Planning for the future.

Finish the statement: The next time that inner
a**hole starts acting up, I will…

_____

_____

_____

_____

_____

_____

_____

_____

_____

_____

_____

_____

_____

WORKSHEET #14

You are NOT your inner a**hole.

That nagging voice is not who you really are. Let's work out how you're different.

My inner a**hole is… | But I am…

WORKSHEET #15

Taking back control.

List everything you plan to do to take back your power from your inner a**hole.

Ex: Every time she starts telling me I can't do this, I'm going to remind myself that this voice is not ME and keep going.

_____

_____

_____

_____

_____

_____

_____

_____

_____

_____

_____

"In the depth of winter, I finally learned that within me lay an infinite summer."

-Albert Camus

For more tips, tools, and resources to help you with sobriety, visit https://soberish.co. You're not alone.

Made in the USA
Middletown, DE
02 October 2020